The Three Birds

A Story for Children about the Loss of a Loved One

by Marinus van den Berg
illustrated by Sandra Ireland

Magination Press · New York

Library of Congress Cataloging-in-Publication Data

Berg, Marinus van den, 1947–
   [Drie vogels. English]
   The three birds : a story for children about the loss of a loved
one / by Marinus van den Berg ; illustrated by Sandra Ireland.
     p.   cm.
   Includes bibliographical references.
   ISBN 0-945354-59-2
   1. Loss (Psychology) in children—Juvenile literature. 2. Death—
Psychological aspects—Juvenile literature. 3. Parents—Death—
Psychological aspects—Juvenile literature.   I. Ireland, Sandra.
II. Title.
BF723.L68B3713   1994
155.9′37—dc20   93-38734
                                         CIP

This edition introduction and end matter © 1994 by Magination Press.
First published in 1990 as *De drie vogels* by Uitgeverij J.H. Gotmer/H.J.W. Becht bv,
Haarlem, The Netherlands. Text © 1994 by Marinus van den Berg.
Illustrations © 1990 by Sandra Ireland.

Published by
Magination Press,
an imprint of Brunner/Mazel, Inc.
19 Union Square West
New York, NY 10003

Manufactured in the United States of America

10 9 8 7 6 5 4 3 2 1

Introduction for Parents

Losing someone we love is a painful experience for all of us. For a child, one of the hardest losses is the death of a parent. Many sources of comfort and much time are required before healing can begin. Loving relatives, family friends and counselors all search for ways to ease the grief and fill the gap the loss has left in the daily life of the child.

The sensitive story of *The Three Birds* can be one of the sources of healing. The gentle understanding of the text and the moving illustrations make this a book that children will cherish and keep nearby for reassurance during moments of sadness.

This tender tale does not deal explicitly with events in the child's life or with the child's emotional reaction to them. After first reading the story with a child, on subsequent "readings" sensitive family members and professionals may want to ignore the text for a while and ask the child to describe what he or she thinks each picture is about. This process may elicit many memories of the deceased parent, or other loved one, as well as a wide range of feelings. Experiencing, sharing and discussing these memories and emotions are important steps in accepting and learning to live with the loss.

At the back of this book is a list of resources where family members and professionals can find additional sources of healing for bereaved children.

The Three Birds will offer comfort and hope to children faced with incomprehensible loss, and to the adults who read this book with them.

Once upon a time, there was a young bird who knew just what she wanted in life. She found her very own place in the branches and let no one chase her away. She whistled her own song, and no one could

change her tune. She flew wherever she wished. When other birds
sought shelter from a storm near her special place, the little bird chose to
fly on alone.

The little bird grew strong and wise, and one day she made up her mind

to leave the nest. She was not afraid — she could look after herself.

She enjoyed being free, and yet . . . sometimes . . . sometimes, she felt just a little bit lonely. Then she met another bird. He was handsome

and kind. She felt happy just sitting close to him.

Before long, they knew they were made for each other. They soared

through the skies together. At night, they cuddled up on the same branch.

Soon, they built a nest for a baby bird of their own. When the baby was

born, they were the happiest three birds in the world.

The new baby soon grew big and strong. But about the time it had
learned to fly a little, something strange happened. The mother bird, who

loved freedom so much, could not fly as well as she had once done.
Her wings felt heavy, and she had to rest often.

Then one day, she could fly no more. The father bird sat with her all the

time, quiet and sad. The baby bird could not understand what was wrong.

One day, the sick bird became very still. Sadly, she had died.

That meant the father bird and the baby bird would have to go on alone.

"Where is my mother now?" asked the baby bird.
"She is living in the sun," said the father bird. "It is warm there, and she can fly again."

"Can we go there, too?" asked the baby bird.
"No," said the father bird. "It is not yet time for us. Only a bird
that can no longer fly in our world can live in the sun."

"But the sun keeps us warm. We will look for the warmth, you and I,"
said the father bird.

Then the father bird and the baby bird spread their wings and flew away, together.

Resources

Aliki. *The Two of Them.* New York: Greenwillow Books, 1979. About the love between a young girl and her grandfather and how she copes with his illness and death.

Fassler, J. *My Grandpa Died Today.* New York: Human Sciences Press, 1983. Young boy experiences his sadness over his loss, then goes on to play with friends without guilt.

Grollman, E.A. *Talking About Death: A Dialogue Between Parent and Child.* Boston: Beacon Press, 1990. How to talk to children at different developmental stages.

Heegaard, M. *When Someone Very Special Dies.* Minneapolis: Woodland Press, 1991. A coloring/work book to help children express and cope with feelings of loss and grief.

Holden, D. *Gran-Gran's Best Trick: A Story for Children Who Have Lost Someone They Love.* New York: Magination Press, 1989. A child copes with her grandfather's illness and death from cancer.

Junneau, B.F. *Sad But O.K.: My Daddy Died Today: A Child's View of Death.* Grass Valley, CA: Blue Dolphin Press, 1988.

Krementz, J. *How It Feels When a Parent Dies.* New York: Alfred A. Knopf, 1988. Short narratives written by children of all ages.

LeShan, E. *Learning to Say Good-Bye: When a Parent Dies.* New York: Avon Books. For teens: How to deal with death, adults, and their own feelings about going on living.

Mellonie, B. & Ingpen, R. *Lifetimes: A Beautiful Way to Explain Death to Children.* New York: Bantam Books, 1983. Uses the life cycles of plants and animals to show how humans have life cycles also.

Mills, J.C. *Gentle Willow: A Story for Children About Dying.* New York: Magination Press, 1993. Helps children cope with their own life-threatening illness or with the death of someone they care about.

Stein, S.B. *About Dying: An Open Family Book for Parents and Children Together.* New York: Walker and Co., 1974.

Thomas, J.R. *Saying Good-bye to Grandma.* New York: Clarion Books, 1988. Shows children reacting unselfconsciously to the experience of a funeral.

For Lori, with love

Tall Tales are happy, rollicking stories based upon America's great treasury of folklore. Many famous characters step from the pages of these books and beckon young readers to join them in wondrous adventures and giant feats sure to delight all children.

Gay, carefree pictures perfectly illustrate the text. These imaginative, easy-to-read stories give young readers a hearty welcome to the magic realm of books.

How Davy Crockett Got a Bearskin Coat

by Wyatt Blassingame

illustrated by Mimi Korach

GARRARD PUBLISHING COMPANY
CHAMPAIGN, ILLINOIS

How Davy Crockett
Got a Bearskin Coat

One morning Mrs. Crockett was cooking breakfast. She needed more wood for her stove.

"Davy," she told her husband, "bring me some wood from the woodpile."

Davy looked out of the window. The first snow of the winter was on the ground.

"It's cold out there," Davy said.

"Put on your fur coat," Mrs. Crockett replied.

Davy opened the closet door. Out flew a moth as big as a buzzard. Then another moth flew out, and another. The room was filled with giant moths.

"Look out!" Davy yelled. "Look what's been eating my coat!"

"Help!" Mrs. Crockett shouted as a large moth landed on the end of her nose.

She picked up her broom and
waved it wildly.
"Get out of here!"

She knocked over a chair and broke some dishes on the shelf. Davy stood by and watched her while she shooed all the moths out of the cabin.

Then he put on the moth-eaten fur coat. He plodded through the snow to the woodpile.

While he was picking up some wood, he saw a raccoon asleep in the top of a tree. The 'coon looked warm and comfortable in his fur coat.

"Oh ho!" said Davy to himself. "I know what I'm going to do after breakfast."

Davy took the wood back to the house. Soon he was eating a breakfast of pancakes and honey.

"Make some more pancakes and honey for my lunch," Davy told his wife. "I'm going hunting."

Davy took his gun down from
the wall. He put a paper bag filled
with pancakes and honey in his
pocket. Then he called his dog from
under the stove.

"Come on, Fearless," Davy said.
"I'm going to shoot enough 'coons
to make me a fur coat."

Davy opened the cabin door. Fearless put one paw out in the snow and pulled it right back. The snow was too cold.

The dog crawled back under the stove.

"All right. I'll go hunting by myself," Davy said.

So he went out toward the woodpile. The big 'coon was still in the tree. Davy took careful aim.

Just then the 'coon moved. He looked down at Davy aiming the gun. "Now wait just a minute!" the 'coon said. "Is your name Davy Crockett?"

Davy was so surprised to hear the 'coon talk that he dropped his gun in the snow.

"That's right," Davy said. "How did you know?"

The 'coon stood up on his back feet and waved a front paw.

"Why, everybody knows Davy
Crockett is the best shot in the
world," he said. "So I won't even
try to run. I'll just come down."

The 'coon climbed slowly down
the tree.

"Are you going to eat me for
dinner?" he asked.

Davy was pleased because the 'coon said he was the best shot in the world.

"I was going to use your skin for a fur coat," he said. "But I never met a 'coon that could talk. So I'm going to let you go."

"Thank you," the 'coon said.

Davy bent to pick up his gun.

"I wouldn't make a very good fur coat," the 'coon said. "So I'll be going." He went up the tree so fast he was at the top in less than a second. He jumped into the next tree. Before Davy could count to five, that 'coon was out of sight.

Davy scratched his head. Then
he went on hunting.

He saw a squirrel, but he
didn't shoot it. It would take too
many squirrels to make a fur coat.

Then Davy saw a rabbit.

But he'd need a lot of rabbits
to make a fur coat.

Davy saw a red bird, a blue
bird, and a black bird.

But nobody could make a fur
coat out of birds.

Just then Davy saw a bear sitting in the snow. The bear's fur was thick and warm. In fact, the bear was fanning himself to keep cool.

"That bear is just my size," Davy thought. "He will make me a fine fur coat."

Quietly Davy raised his gun.

He took careful aim. He pulled the trigger.

Nothing happened.

Davy pulled harder and harder. Still nothing happened.

Then Davy remembered that he had dropped his gun in the snow. The powder must be wet so the gun wouldn't fire.

Suddenly the big bear smelled Davy's lunch bag full of pancakes and honey. It made him hungry. He looked around and saw Davy.

"That man smells like pancakes and honey," the bear thought.

There was nothing this bear liked better. He smacked his lips.

"I'll just eat this man and his pancakes and honey for lunch," he thought.

With a growl the bear rushed toward Davy.

Davy dropped his gun and ran. The bear ran right behind him.

In front of Davy was a big
snowbank.

It was too high to jump over.
And there was no time to run
around it.

Davy didn't have time to think.
He just ran straight into the
snowbank. He was running so fast
he made a tunnel right through it.
The bear was close behind him.

Davy ran up one mountain. He ran down another.

The bear was still on his heels.

Halfway up the next mountain Davy saw a hollow tree. There was a big hole near the bottom. There was a smaller hole above the big one.

"If I can lose this bear for just a minute," Davy thought, "I can hide in that tree."

When Davy got to the tree, he jumped quickly behind it.

The bear was running too fast to stop. He ran right on up the mountain.

VINELAND PUBLIC SCHOOL

Davy jumped into the big hole
at the bottom of the tree. He
looked out of the little hole.

The bear knew that he had
lost Davy. He turned and came
running back down the mountain.

He sniffed all around looking for Davy.

The bear smelled the pancakes and honey. He knew that they were nearby, but he couldn't see Davy. The bear ran close to the tree.

Quickly Davy reached out and grabbed the bear's tail. He pulled it through the small hole in the tree and tied a knot.

The knot in the bear's tail was too big to pass through the knot-hole in the tree. The bear was running too fast to stop. When he reached the end of his tail, there was a loud noise—POW!

The bear ran right out of his skin. He left it hanging on the tree.

The bear stopped running. He knew he had lost his fur. He was cold, and he thought that he must look funny without his coat.

"What will I do now?" thought
the bear. "I can't go around like
this. All the other bears will laugh
at me."

The bear found a cave to hide
in. The cave was dark and warm.

The bear lay down and went
to sleep.

After the bear went away,
Davy came out of the tree. He put
on the bear's coat. The thick fur
was warm and comfortable in the
cold air.

Davy went home to show off
his new coat. He wanted his wife
to see how well it fit.

Inside the cave the bear was asleep. He slept all winter. While he slept he grew a beautiful, new, lightweight fur coat. It was just heavy enough for spring when he awoke.

There was only one difference between the bear's new coat and his old one.

The new fur coat had a very short tail.

And ever since that time, bears have had short tails.

MEET THE AUTHOR

A native of Alabama, Wyatt Blassingame has been a professional writer most of his life, having written adult fiction and non-fiction as well as many juvenile books. After three years in the navy during World War II with Air Combat Intelligence and brief jobs teaching, he began to write. Mr. Blassingame has had hundreds of magazine stories and articles published, one of which won the Benjamin Franklin Award as the best short story of 1956. He and his family live on Anna Maria, an island off the gulf coast of Florida.

MEET THE ARTIST

Mimi Korach was born in New York, was raised in Connecticut, and attended Yale University Art School. During World War II she did aeronautical drafting for a time; then she went to Europe for the USO. There she sketched thousands of GI's in hospitals. In private life she is Mrs. Bert Lesser and the mother of a son and a daughter. In addition to illustrating books for children, Mrs. Lesser has a studio in New Rochelle, New York, where she does portraits and easel painting.